THE UNIVERSE

THE UNIVERSE

PAST, PRESENT, AND FUTURE

by David J. Darling

Illustrated by Jeanette Swofford

DILLON PRESS, INC.   MINNEAPOLIS, MINNESOTA

Photographs are reproduced through the courtesy of AT&T Bell Laboratories, Cerro Tololo Inter-American Observatory, Hale Observatories, Kitt Peak National Observatory, the National Aeronautics and Space Administration, and the Palomar Observatory of the California Institute of Technology.

Dillon Press, Inc., 242 Portland Avenue South
Minneapolis, Minnesota 55415

Printed in the United States of America

Library of Congress Cataloging in Publication Data

Darling, David J.
    The Universe : past, present and future.

    Bibliography: p.
    Includes index.
    Summary: Explains the Big Bang theory of the formation of the universe and discusses its possible continued growth.
        1. Cosmology—Juvenile literature [1. Universe]
I. Title.
QB983.D37   1985   523.1   84-23068
ISBN 0-87518-286-0

2   3   4   5   6   7   8   9   10   91   90   89   88   87   86   85

Contents

Universe Facts 7

Questions and Answers about the Universe 8

1 Our Journey through Space 11
2 Red Shifts and Galaxies 17
3 Explosion! 23
4 The Universe to Come 31
5 At the Edge of Space 39

Appendix A: Discover for Yourself 43

Appendix B: Amateur Astronomy Groups in the United States, Canada, and Great Britain 46

Glossary 47

Suggested Reading 53

Index 54

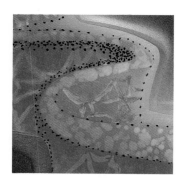

Universe Facts

Age: About 15 billion years

Size: Scientists do not know if the universe has a definite size. It is expanding, and right now it may be about 30 billion light-years across

Most Distant Objects: Quasars, which may be more than 10 billion light-years from the earth

Number of Galaxies: Astronomers have discovered at least as many galaxies in the universe as there are stars in our galaxy, the Milky Way. The Galaxy has more than 100 billion stars

Makeup: The universe contains all the matter, light, and other forms of radiation and energy that have been discovered, as well as everything else that exists somewhere in space and time

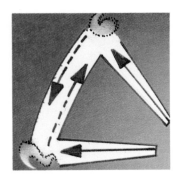

Questions & Answers About the Universe

Q. Is the universe changing?
A. Yes. The universe is getting bigger, and the objects within it are growing older. Galaxies today, for example, appear different than those of long ago.

Q. How close to the exact time of the Big Bang will our present theories work?
A. About one ten million trillion trillion trillionth of a second! To go beyond this point, to the Big Bang itself, scientists must discover how gravity works at the very highest of energies.

Q. Will we ever be able to see the Big Bang by looking far enough into space?
A. Not in ordinary light. Because material in the early universe absorbed light, it would stop us from actually "seeing" the Big Bang. However, very high energy waves did manage to escape, and we see these today, much red-shifted, as the cosmic microwave background.

Q. Will we ever be able to see the first galaxies being formed?

A. This may be possible. One of the exciting hopes for the Space Telescope, to be launched in 1986, is that it may show the earliest galaxies and quasars shortly after they were formed.

Q. Are all of the galaxies in space moving away from us?

A. Yes, except for a handful within our Local Group of galaxies. The Local Group is held together by the gravity of its members. Several galaxies in the Local Group have "blue shifts" that show they are moving towards us.

Q. Why is the universe like a "time machine"?

A. Light from objects far away takes longer to reach us than light from objects close by because light can only travel at a certain speed: 186,282 miles per second. The result is that the farther we look into space, the farther we look back in time.

THE EARTH, PHOTOGRAPHED FROM AN APOLLO SPACECRAFT

1 Our Journey Through Space

Did you know that we are all riding aboard a high-speed spaceship? That spaceship is the planet earth. Let's find out where it is and where it's taking us.

Earth is one of nine planets that, along with some smaller objects and our neighborhood star, the sun, make up the **solar system.*** We travel around the sun at a distance of about 93 **million** miles (150 million kilometers) and at a speed of 66,000 miles per hour (106,000 kilometers per hour). Still, this journey is just the smallest of our motions through space.

To us, the solar system seems huge. Pluto, the most distant planet, is more than 3½ **billion** miles (5½ billion kilometers) away from the sun. Yet, the solar system is just a tiny speck in the vast reaches of space.

In fact, the sun is just an ordinary star inside a giant star city. We call this city the **Galaxy** and it contains more than 100 billion stars.

Beyond the solar system, distances become hard to imagine. They are so great that scientists measure them, not in miles or kilometers, but in **light-years.** One light-year is the distance that light, traveling at 186,000 miles per second (300,000 kilometers per second), covers in a year—about 6 **trillion** miles (9½ trillion kilometers).

*Words in **bold type** are explained in the glossary at the end of this book.

These drawings show the solar system as seen looking toward earth from the moon (bottom); the relative sizes of the planets and their distances from the sun (middle); the orbits of the planets (top center). The Milky Way Galaxy (top left) is also shown.

Our galaxy, often called the Milky Way, is at least 100,000 light-years across. Shaped like a pinwheel, and slowly turning, it is so big that it takes us 230 million years, moving at 136 miles per second (220 kilometers per second) to make just one trip all the way around!

How could anything be bigger than the Galaxy? Yet, compared with the whole of space, our own star city is as small as a drop of water in the ocean.

The Universe Beyond

Astronomers have discovered that our galaxy is not alone. Together with 30, mostly smaller, neighboring star cities, it forms a **cluster of galaxies** called the **Local Group.**

In fact, the Local Group itself is still quite small. Mea-

Viewed from the outside, this galaxy in the constellation of Pavo probably looks much like our own Milky Way. The photograph was taken by a powerful telescope at the Cerro Tololo Inter-American Observatory.

suring just 5 million light-years across, it is held together mainly by the **gravity** of its two largest members—our own galaxy and the slightly larger Andromeda Galaxy. Beyond the Local Group are other clusters containing hundreds, or even thousands, of galaxies.

Throughout the whole of space, scientists think there may be as many as a hundred billion star cities. Most are arranged, like our own, into clusters. In turn, these clusters may be grouped into **superclusters,** or clusters of clusters of galaxies. The Local Group, for example, seems to belong to the **Local Supercluster,** whose center is about 65 million light-years away.

Recently, astronomers have found huge parts of space where there appear to be no galaxies at all. These giant gaps, or voids, may be hundreds of millions of light-

This photo shows a large cluster of galaxies in the constellation of Coma Berenices. Astronomers have discovered that clusters of galaxies may be grouped into superclusters—clusters of clusters of galaxies.

14

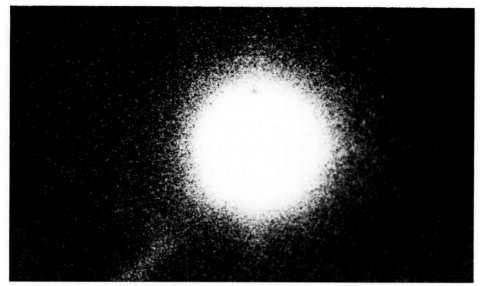

Quasars, such as 3C-273 shown here, are the most distant objects yet observed in the universe—from 7 to 12 billion light-years away from earth.

years across. Like the holes in a sponge, they are separated only by thin "sheets" of **matter.** In fact, most of space may be completely empty.

Astronomers have discovered galaxies as far as 7 billion light-years away from earth. Beyond that, they have found strange objects called **quasars** as far as 12 billion light-years away. This means that, if everything were squeezed down so that the solar system fitted inside the dot over this *i*, then the most distant objects known would still be 5 million miles (8 million kilometers) away!

We have a name for all of space and everything that it contains—the **universe.** It is this largest and most amazing of places that we're now about to explore.

DOPPLER SHIFT

OBJECT MOVING
TOWARD US

LIGHT WAVES

OBJECT'S COLOR
SPECTRUM

LIGHT WAVES

OBJECT MOVING
AWAY FROM US

2 Red Shifts and Galaxies

Have you ever heard the note of a siren change as an ambulance or fire truck speeds by? The siren goes from a higher note, when it's coming towards you, to a lower note when it's going away.

Sound is really made of waves moving through the air. If the waves are bunched together, as they are when a siren approaches, then the pitch of the sound you hear is higher. If the waves are more spread out, as when the siren moves away, then the pitch is lower. This change in sound is known as the **Doppler effect,** after the scientist who first described it.

In fact, the Doppler effect works just the same for light as it does for sound because light, too, is made up of waves. When something that is giving off light moves towards us, the light waves we see from it are crowded more closely together. Since the crowded waves appear bluer, the result is called a **blue shift.** When, on the other hand, we look at light coming from something that is moving away, we see the light waves as more spread out. Since the spread out waves seem redder, the result is a **red shift.** Scientists call either kind of shift—red or blue—a **Doppler shift.**

The amount by which light from an object is "Doppler-shifted" depends on the speed at which the object is either coming towards us or going away from us. By measuring Doppler shifts, then, scientists can discover how distant objects in space are moving.

Astronomers began by looking at the Doppler shifts of nearby stars. They found, as we might expect, that about half of them are red and half are blue. This means that, within our own galaxy, about the same number of stars are going away from us as are coming towards us. What's more, their speeds are quite low, usually less than 50 miles per second (80 kilometers per second).

Then, in 1912, astronomer Vesto Slipher took a first look at the Doppler shifts of faint, whirlpool-shaped patches of light that were called spiral nebulas. These were thought to be clouds of gas inside our own galaxy.

Astronomer Vesto Slipher took a first look at faint, whirlpool-shaped patches of light known then as "spiral nebulas." Later, Edwin Hubble discovered that the "spiral nebulas" were really spiral galaxies, such as the one shown here in the constellation of Pisces.

Altogether, Slipher measured the Doppler shifts of 15 spiral nebulas. What he found was very surprising. Of the 15, most had red shifts, showing that they were moving away from earth. But more surprising still, their speeds were very high. The spiral nebulas were flying away at an average speed of several hundred miles per second!

Galaxies in Flight

For scientists these results were puzzling. If spiral nebulas really were inside our own galaxy, then why did they move so differently from the stars?

In the 1920s, American astronomer Edwin Hubble helped provide the answer. Using what was then the largest telescope in the world, on top of Mount Wilson in California, he took the first close-up photographs of Slipher's

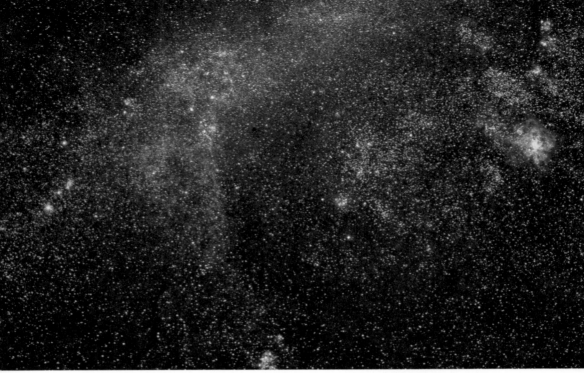

The large Magellanic cloud is an irregular galaxy located in the constellation of Dorado. Unlike spiral and elliptical galaxies, irregular galaxies have no definite shape.

spiral nebulas. To his surprise, the pictures showed that spiral "nebulas" were **spiral galaxies!** What's more, there were other types of star cities, called **elliptical galaxies** and **irregular galaxies,** that were scattered in huge numbers across space.

Through careful studies, Hubble was able to measure the distance to some of these galaxies. A few, such as the great spiral in Andromeda about 2 million light-years away, turned out to be quite close by. Others lay tens or hundreds of millions of light-years away.

Hubble looked especially at the distances to galaxies for which Slipher had already measured the red shift. In almost every case, he found, the more distant the galaxy, the greater was its red shift. Galaxies far away were racing from us faster than those near by! Only in the case of

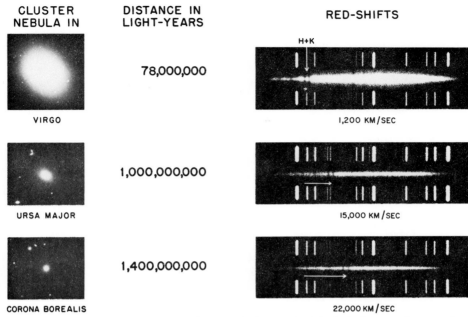

CLUSTER NEBULA IN	DISTANCE IN LIGHT-YEARS	RED-SHIFTS
VIRGO	78,000,000	1,200 KM/SEC
URSA MAJOR	1,000,000,000	15,000 KM/SEC
CORONA BOREALIS	1,400,000,000	22,000 KM/SEC

This chart shows photos of three cluster nebulas on the left, their distance from earth in light-years in the center, and their red shifts in kilometers per second on the right.

galaxies within the Local Group was this not true.

Later, scientists found still more distant galaxies with still greater red shifts. Then, in the 1960s, they found the most distant objects of all—quasars.

Today, we know of quasars that lie more than 10 billion light-years away. Their enormous red shifts mean that they are flying away from us at more than nine-tenths the speed of light! Why are the galaxies and quasars in flight?

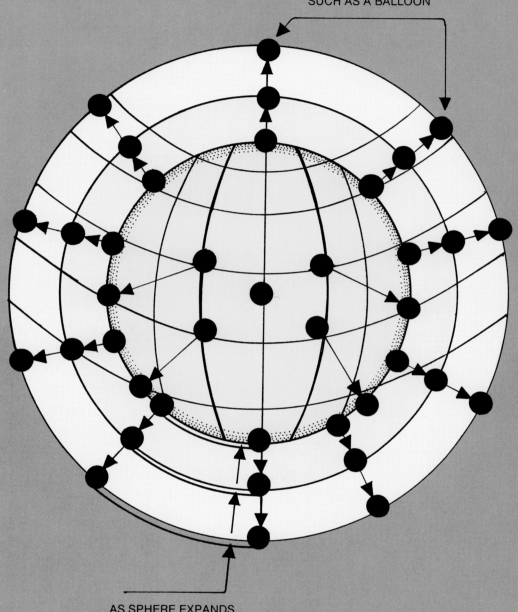

GALAXIES ON SURFACE
OF EXPANDING SPHERE
SUCH AS A BALLOON

AS SPHERE EXPANDS,
DISTANCE BETWEEN
GALAXIES INCREASES

3 Explosion!

Imagine a balloon whose surface has been painted with spots. Pretend that one of the spots is our galaxy, and other spots are other galaxies. Now, start to blow up the balloon. What happens? The balloon's surface stretches, growing larger and larger. At the same time, the spots move apart. Looking outwards from any one of the spots, we would see all the others moving away from us—the greater their distance, the greater their speed.

This pattern of growth is exactly what Hubble found when he looked at the Doppler shifts of distant galaxies! In fact, our universe is very much like a spotted balloon. The spots are galaxies, and the rubber surface of the balloon is space. Just like a balloon that's being blown up, our universe is growing in size, too!

The Big Bang

Since the universe is growing, most scientists believe that it was once much smaller than it is today. Long ago, the galaxies must have been much closer together.

If we go back far enough, say the scientists, we reach a time when all of the matter in the universe was squashed within the tiniest of spaces. Although we can't imagine it, this space was smaller than a pinhead but

These pictures represent an artist's view of how the universe has changed over 15 billion years. On the left-hand page, the powerful explosion called the Big Bang occurs, and hydrogen and helium form large clouds. To the right, gravity forces the

weighed as much as ten billion trillion stars!

Then, there was an incredibly powerful explosion. Scientists call this the **Big Bang** and think that it happened about 15 billion years ago. During the Big Bang, all the matter that we see today in galaxies, stars, even our own bodies, was thrown outwards at high speed. Such was the strength of the explosion that, even now, space and everything in it is still moving apart.

The Universe after the Big Bang

Scientists have traced what the universe may have been like to within just one ten million trillion trillion trillionth of a second of the Big Bang itself. Then, space was tiny. It was filled with a fantastically hot, thick "soup." There was no ordinary matter as we know it today. The soup pouring out of the Big Bang was filled with strange particles such as **gravitons** and **quarks.**

As the universe grew, it cooled down. After about three minutes, it was cool enough for pieces of **hydrogen** called **protons** to form. Then, a few minutes later, pieces of **helium,** the next simplest substance, were made.

For millions more years, following the Big Bang, only a slowly cooling, thinning gas of hydrogen and helium filled space. The universe was still very young, and far smaller than it is today.

Then, after about 100 million years, the hydrogen and helium gas began to clump together in huge clouds. These clouds became smaller as their own gravity pulled them inwards. From the big clouds came smaller clouds—the **protogalaxies**—that shrank even faster.

Viewed from the side, a normal spiral galaxy looks much like this one in the constellation of Virgo. It has a bulging middle surrounded by a broader, pancake-shaped disk.

About one billion years after the Big Bang, gas inside some of the protogalaxies became thick enough to form stars. The first of the true galaxies began to shine!

Clues from the Past

How can scientists know that the universe has changed so much over the last 15 billion years? How can they know that there was even a Big Bang at all?

Until quite recently, some scientists thought that the universe might always have been more or less as it is today. Their idea was that as the galaxies moved apart, new matter was made in the spaces between them. This new matter would keep the universe, as seen from any point, about the same forever. It is called the **steady state theory.**

Viewed from above, this normal spiral galaxy in the constellation of Centaurus looks like a giant pinwheel with its long, glowing, spiral-shaped arms.

Now, though, we know of at least two good reasons why the steady state theory is probably wrong. The first is that galaxies long ago appear differently than they do today.

When we look at something far away, we see it not as it is now, but as it was when the light now entering our eyes left its surface. In this way the universe works very much like a time machine. We see, for example, a galaxy that is 10 million light-years away as it was 10 million years ago.

Beyond a distance of one billion light-years, ordinary galaxies are hard to see. Even through our biggest telescopes, they are just faint smudges of light. But some distant galaxies are anything but ordinary.

As astronomers look deeper and deeper into space,

Seyfert galaxies like the one shown above have extremely bright centers and are spiral in shape. They are examples of active galaxies.

they start to see more and more bright, or "active," galaxies. These appear quite different from normal star cities like our own. Some give off huge amounts of **radio waves** and are called **radio galaxies.** Others are spiral shaped, but with very bright centers—the **Seyfert galaxies.** Beyond 5 billion light-years, we start to see the most brilliant objects of all. These are the quasars—perhaps galaxies newly born—so far away that their light set out on its great journey before our world was even made.

The universe of long ago, then, was different than the universe of today. Some galaxies, at least, have grown dimmer with time. Such a change is what we would expect if the universe had been born from an explosion in the distant past.

The Holmdel horn antenna was used by scientists to discover the cosmic microwave background. These microwaves are weak rays of energy that come from all parts of space.

Another recently discovered fact also supports the idea of a Big Bang. It became known in 1965, when scientists first spotted **microwaves**—weak rays of energy—coming from all parts of space. These rays form a **microwave background** that is, almost certainly, the dying echo of the Big Bang itself.

A DISTANT CLUSTER OF GALAXIES

4 The Universe To Come

We have a fairly clear picture of what our universe may have been like in the distant past. Now let's take a look at its future.

For billions more years, the galaxies will continue to fly apart. The distances between them will become much greater than they are today.

At the same time, gravity will gradually work to slow down the growth of the universe. Even galaxies that are millions, or billions, of light-years apart pull on each other through gravity. The big question is: Can the force of gravity in space stop the universe from growing?

A Question of Balance

To find the answer, we must do a very strange thing—we must "weigh" the universe! We must find out how much matter there is in space, because the total weight of all matter determines the strength of gravity. If there is enough matter, then the pull of gravity will be strong enough to halt the growth of the universe. Otherwise, the explosive force of the Big Bang will cause space to continue to grow forever.

In order to weigh the whole universe, we need to weigh both the "bright" matter and the "dark" matter

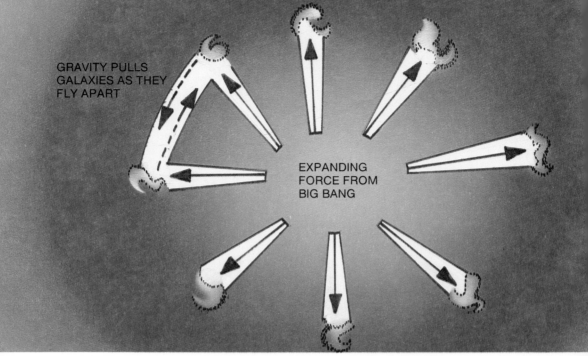

GRAVITY PULLS
GALAXIES AS THEY
FLY APART

EXPANDING
FORCE FROM
BIG BANG

This drawing shows the two main forces in the universe. The outward, explosive force of the Big Bang causes the universe to expand, while gravity works to hold it together. Eventually, scientists believe, the force of gravity will slow down the growth of the universe.

that it contains. Bright matter shines and is found mostly in the form of stars. If we add up all the stars in all the galaxies, we find that they have only about one-thirtieth of the gravity needed to stop the universe from growing forever.

But what of dark matter? Scientists have discovered that as much as nine-tenths of the material in space is in a form that we can't see. Some of it may be at the bottom of **black holes**—regions of space whose gravity is so strong that nothing, not even light, can escape from them. Some may be cold gas that floats in, and around, the galaxies. Some may even be in the form of tiny particles—**neutrinos**—that were thrown out in huge numbers during the Big Bang.

We still don't know if there is enough dark matter to

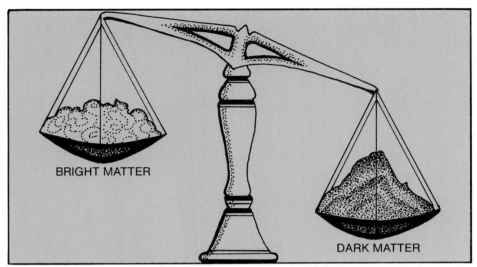

BRIGHT MATTER

DARK MATTER

The bright matter in the universe, shown on the left-hand side of this scale, does not weigh nearly as much as the dark matter, shown on the right. Galaxies and quasars are examples of bright matter, while black holes and neutrinos are examples of dark matter.

overcome the force that has kept the universe growing for 15 billion years. Most scientists think that the universe will probably go on expanding forever. Yet others believe that, in the years to come, more dark matter will be found which will make gravity the strongest force of all.

Possible Futures

Let's look first at what will happen if the universe keeps on growing forever. For billions of years, there will be little change from the universe we know today. The galaxies will continue to move apart.

Then, gradually, all the stars in the galaxies will die. There will be no more new stars made, and space will become a dreary place with hardly any light.

After a much longer time—about a hundred million

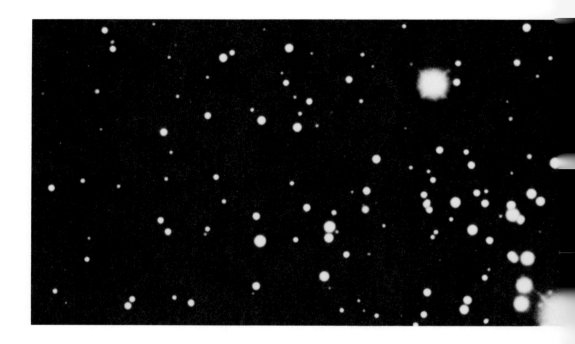

billion years—planets such as earth will escape from their stars. Later still, the once great star cities themselves will start to break up. Dead stars will escape from the galaxies into the spaces between.

In the very distant future, long after the sun and earth have disappeared, huge black holes will roam the universe. They will capture any ordinary matter that remains. Finally, after trillions upon trillions of years, even the black holes will vanish. Then, all that will be left in the vast and still-growing universe will be a thin, cold mixture of tiny particles.

An ever-growing universe means that space is **open,** or has no end. But the universe could end in a much different way. Let's look at what will happen to the universe if gravity can stop it from growing. This would mean that

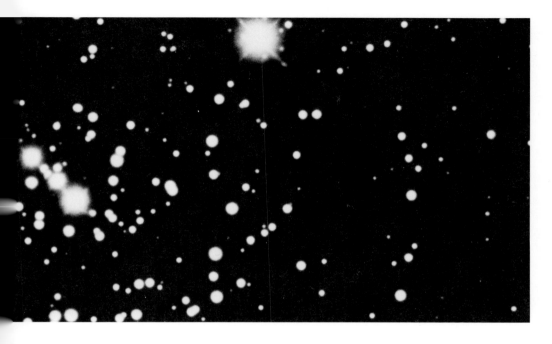

space is **closed,** that it has a limited size.

If gravity is strong enough, after tens or hundreds of billions of years, the tugging between the galaxies will bring them to a halt. The universe will have grown to its greatest size. Then, it will start to shrink!

Slowly at first, the galaxies will begin to pull each other together again. If we could look at their Doppler shifts, we would see that they had turned from red to blue. Then, gradually, the shrinking of the universe will speed up. The galaxies will come together faster and faster.

After a long time, space, and all the matter in it, will meet at a single point. Instead of a Big Bang, there will be a "Big Crunch!" The universe will have returned to the incredibly hot, thick "soup" from which it began.

Could there be another Big Bang after the Big

In this picture, an artist imagines what the universe would be like if gravity were strong enough to cause a "Big Crunch." All of space and the matter in it would come together to form the incredibly hot, thick soup from which the universe began in the Big Bang.

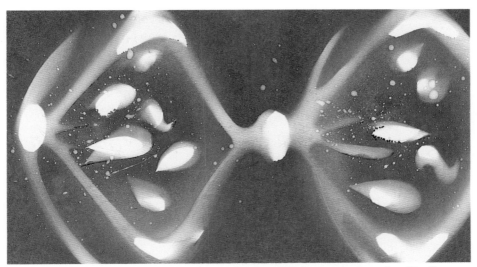

This drawing shows a universe that expands after the explosion of a Big Bang, contracts into a tiny point in a Big Crunch, and then explodes again. In the past, scientists say, the universe may have gone through many Big Bangs and Big Crunches.

Crunch? Is it possible that the universe has been through many Big Bangs and Big Crunches in the past, and that it will go through many more in the future? At present, scientists have no way of knowing what the real beginning and ending of the universe may be.

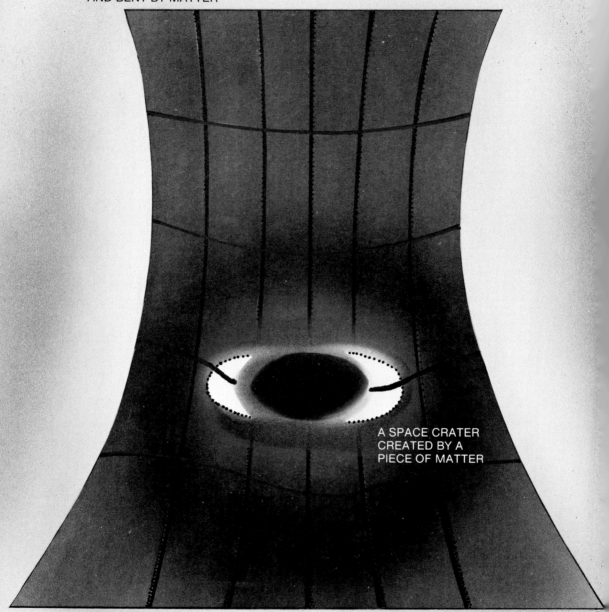

A SECTION OF SPACE
THAT HAS BEEN STRETCHED
AND BENT BY MATTER

A SPACE CRATER
CREATED BY A
PIECE OF MATTER

5 At the Edge of Space

In talking about the universe, we said that space might be "open" or it might be "closed." We also said that space is like the rubber surface of a balloon. Now let's take a closer look at space to find out what it may be like.

Space is very different than we might imagine. It can be stretched and bent. Anything that has **mass**—for example, a planet or a star—causes the space around it to curve. Each piece of matter lies at the bottom of its own "space crater" (see *Appendix A: Discover For Yourself*). Because of all the matter scattered throughout space, the universe as a whole must be curved!

If the universe is curved like the surface of a balloon, then space is closed. In other words, there is enough matter to fold space so that it always has a definite size. A closed universe is one that will, in time, stop growing, and then shrink back again to a Big Crunch.

On the other hand, the universe may be curved something like the surface of a saddle. Then, space would be open and would stretch away in every direction forever. Galaxies in such a universe would always move apart.

These ideas are very strange and perhaps hard to understand. But they do help us to answer an important question: Where does space end?

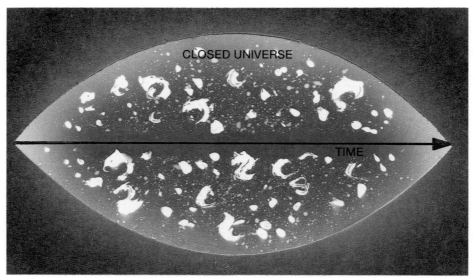

CLOSED UNIVERSE

TIME

In this picture, an artist represents a "closed" universe. Such a universe always has a definite size and will, in time, stop growing and shrink until it reaches its tiny starting point. Time passes through in what is called a "positive space-time curvature."

The answer is that space has no end. If the universe has a surface like that of a balloon, then we could travel all the way around it and finally come back to the place where we started. If the universe is "saddle-shaped," we could journey through it forever. Whatever its form, we would not come to an end or an edge.

Using balloons and saddles is a good way to picture how our universe may be shaped. Yet, in fact, the universe is curved in a way that we can never really imagine. It is curved in what scientists call the **fourth dimension,** an extra dimension to the three—length, width, and height—that we already know.

Other Universes

We can never find an edge to our universe. And, for

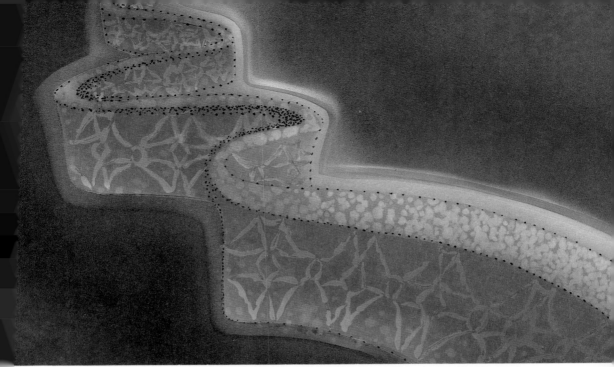

Some scientists believe that there may be other universes unlike our own that formed during the Big Bang. In the picture above, an artist imagines a universe in which hot sheets of gases move with a whiplike motion as energy produced creates heat and movement.

the same reason, we can never see "outside" it. But is it possible that there are other universes beyond our own?

Some scientists now think that, during the Big Bang, not just one, but many, universes were made. In the beginning, space may have foamed and frothed like boiling water in a pan. Each bubble that broke free may then have become a separate universe, as big today as our own.

It may be many years before we know whether or not this bold new idea is correct. Perhaps we will never know for sure. Still, it is exciting to think about. Each of the many universes would be quite different. Could it be that only ours has galaxies, stars, planets, and life?

The more we learn about the universe around us, the more it fascinates us. Past, present, and future, it holds countless mysteries that we are only beginning to unfold.

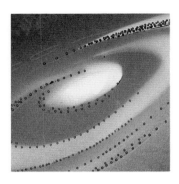

Appendix A:
Discover For Yourself

1. *Measure an Expanding Universe*

For this project, you will need a balloon, a tape measure, a felt-tip pen, paper, and the help of a friend.

Blow the balloon up until it measures about four inches across. Then, while your friend holds the neck of the balloon to stop air escaping, mark the surface of the balloon with six evenly-spaced dots. The balloon's surface is now a model universe and the dots model galaxies inside it.

Circle one of the dots. This will represent the Milky Way—the galaxy in which we live. Label each of the other galaxies with a number, one through five.

On a sheet of paper, make four headings as follows: "Galaxy," "Distance Then," "Distance Now," and "Speed." Under "Galaxy," write down the numbers one through five. Measure the distances from the circled dot (your home galaxy) to each of the numbered dots, and record these values under "Distance Then."

Next, make your model universe grow bigger, just as the real universe is expanding. Blow the balloon up until it is about eight inches across. Measure the distances to all the numbered galaxies again, and write down these new values in the column headed "Distance Now." In the final column, headed "Speed," write down the difference between "Distance Then" and "Distance Now" for each galaxy.

Now, make a chart of your results to show "Distance Now" versus "Speed" for each model galaxy. What is the shape of your chart? What does this tell you?

American astronomer Edwin Hubble was the first to draw such a chart for galaxies in our real universe. Find out more about his work and discover what scientists mean by "Hubble's Law" and the "Hubble constant."

2. *Explore Curved Space*

As with space in the real universe, the surface of your balloon is curved.

Begin at the circled dot and head outwards into "balloon space," drawing a path as straight as possible with your pen. Continue onwards, never straying to the right or left. What happens?

Our own universe may be curved in just the same way as a balloon. In this case, it would be "closed." A spaceship trying to travel forever in a straight line would, in time, go all the way around the universe and return to its starting point!

Appendix B:
Amateur Astronomy Groups
in the United States,
Canada, and Great Britain

For information or resource materials about the subjects covered in this book, contact your local astronomy group, science museum, or planetarium. You may also write to one of the national amateur astronomy groups listed below.

United States

The Astronomical League
Donald Archer,
   Executive Secretary
P.O. Box 12821
Tucson, Arizona 85732

American Association of
   Variable Star Astronomers
187 Concord Avenue
Cambridge, Massachusetts 02138

Great Britain

Junior Astronomical Society
58 Vaughan Gardens
Ilford
Essex IG1 3PD England

British Astronomical Assoc.
Burlington House
Piccadilly
London W1V 0NL England

Canada

The Royal Astronomical Society of Canada
La Société Royale d'Astronomie du Canada
Rosemary Freeman, Executive Secretary
136 Dupont Street
Toronto, Ontario M5R 1V2

Glossary

Big Bang—the great explosion in which, scientists believe, our universe was born. It probably happened about 15 billion years ago
billion—a thousand million. Written as 1,000,000,000
black hole—a region of space whose gravity is so strong that nothing, not even light, can escape.
blue shift—a change in color of an object, making it seem bluer. It happens when an object that is giving off light moves towards us

closed space—since the space we live in is curved, it must either fold back on itself (like the surface of a balloon) or stretch away forever (like the surface of a saddle). A space that folds back on itself is said to be closed
cluster of galaxies—a group of galaxies, with from a few dozen to more than a thousand members, that is held together by gravity

Doppler effect—see *Doppler shift*
Doppler shift—the change

47

in pitch (of sound) or of color (of light) caused when an object that is giving off waves moves either towards us or away from us

elliptical galaxy—a type of galaxy that is round or oval in shape

fourth dimension—a direction in space that we cannot imagine. It points in a different way from the length, width, and height that we know

galaxy—a star city, con-taining billions of stars

Galaxy—the star city in which we live. It is spiral in shape and contains more than 100 billion suns like our own

graviton—the smallest possible "piece" of gravity. Gravitons are so tiny and weak that they have never been seen, but there may be countless numbers of them throughout space

gravity—the force by which all objects pull on all other objects. Gravity will be important in determining the future of the universe

helium—the second lightest, and second most common substance in the universe

hydrogen—the lightest and most common substance of all. It is the "fuel" from which the stars make heat and light

irregular galaxy—a galaxy that has no definite shape

light-year—the distance traveled by light in one year. It is equal to about 6 trillion miles (9½ trillion kilometers)

Local Group—the small cluster of about thirty galaxies to which our own galaxy belongs

Local Supercluster—the supercluster to which the Local Group may belong

mass—the amount of matter in a body as measured by its ability to stay at rest or move in the same direction

matter—anything that can have weight and takes up space

microwave background—the microwave "glow" that shines on the earth from all

49

directions in space. Scientists believe that it is energy from the Big Bang that has gone through a great redshift during its long journey

microwaves—weak rays of energy. Microwaves are a form of radio wave

million—a thousand thousand. Written as 1,000,000

neutrino—a tiny, little-known particle, huge numbers of which travel through space. Neutrinos, if they weigh anything at all, may make up most of the weight of the universe

open space—space that is curved, but which stretches away endlessly in all directions. Our universe may be open, in which case it may be shaped something like the surface of a saddle

protogalaxy—a galaxy in the making. Scientists think that protogalaxies formed billions of years ago from clouds of hydrogen and helium

proton—a tiny particle. Protons are pieces of hydrogen that fuse in the cores of stars and give off great amounts of energy

quark—a building block of other particles, such as the proton. Quarks are not found alone today, but at the time of the Big Bang they may have swarmed everywhere in space

quasar—the brightest, most distant kind of object known. It seems now that quasars may be the very bright centers of newly formed galaxies

radio galaxy—a type of galaxy that gives off an unusually large amount of radio waves

radio waves—weak, invisible rays of energy that are much like light and heat

red shift—a change in color of an object, making it seem redder. A red shift happens when an object that is giving off light moves away from us

Seyfert galaxy—a strange spiral galaxy that gives off huge amounts of energy from a small, starlike center

solar system—the small part of space in which we live. It includes the sun and all the objects that go around it

spiral galaxy—a galaxy from whose center come bright, spiraling arms. The Galaxy we live in is a spiral galaxy

steady state theory—the idea that the universe may not appear to change with time. Instead of a Big Bang, this theory says that matter slowly "leaks" into space, replacing the matter lost as the galaxies move apart

supercluster—a cluster of clusters of galaxies

trillion—a thousand billion. Written as 1,000,000,000,000

universe—all of the space around us and everything that it contains

Suggested Reading

Apfel, Necia H. *It's All Relative: Einstein's Theory of Relativity.* New York: Lothrop, Lee, and Shepard, 1981.
What is the theory of relativity? Why is it so important in our understanding of the universe today? In providing the answers, this book explores many strange ideas such as curved space, black holes, and the shape of the universe. (Advanced)

Asimov, Isaac. *How Did We Find Out About: the Universe?* New York: Walker, 1983.
A history of the discovery of our universe from Galileo to the Space Telescope. (Intermediate)

Darling, David. "Universe: Time Zero." *Astronomy,* November 1980, pp. 14-22.
An imaginary journey aboard a time machine to the universe as it was a few moments after the Big Bang. (Advanced)

Fisher, David. E. *The Creation of the Universe.* Indianapolis: Bobbs-Merrill, 1977.
The Big Bang theory, the importance of gravity, and the work of scientists such as Newton and Einstein are described in this book dealing with the origins of the universe. (Advanced)

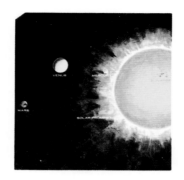

 Index

Andromeda Galaxy, 13, 20

Big Bang, 23-26, 29, 31-32, 35, 37, 39, 41
Big Crunch, 35, 37, 39
black holes, 32, 34
blue shift, 17-18, 35
"bright" matter, 31-32

clusters, 13

"dark" matter, 31-33
Doppler effect, 17
Doppler shift, 17-19, 23, 35

earth, 11, 34
elliptical galaxies, 20

galaxies, cluster of, 12-13

Galaxy, the, 11-12
gravitons, 25
gravity, 13, 25, 31-35

helium, 25
Hubble, Edwin, 19-20, 23
hydrogen, 25

irregular galaxies, 20

light-years, 11-13, 15, 20, 27-28
Local Group, galaxies of, 12-13, 21
Local Supercluster, 13

mass, 39
microwave background, 29
microwaves, 29

Milky Way, 12

neutrinos, 32

planets, 11, 39, 41
Pluto, 11
protogalaxies, 25-26
protons, 25

quarks, 25
quasars, 15, 21, 28

radio galaxies, 28
radio waves, 28
red shift, 17-21, 35

Seyfert galaxies, 28
Slipher, Vesto, 18-20
solar system, 11

sound, 17
space: closed, 34-35; "craters" in, 39; empty, 15; open, 34, 39
spiral nebulas, 18-20
star cities, 11-12, 20, 28, 34
stars, 11, 18-19, 24, 26, 33, 39, 41
steady state theory, 26-27
sun, 11, 34
superclusters, 13

universe: curved, 39-40; fourth dimension of, 40; growth of, 23-26, 28-29, 31-34; shrinking of, 34-35, 37, 39; weight of, 31

voids, 13